MOOT POINTS

MOOT POINTS

Deranged Drawings by J. C. Duffy

ADDISON-WESLEY PUBLISHING COMPANY

Reading, Massachusetts · Menlo Park, California
London · Amsterdam · Don Mills, Ontario · Sydney

Library of Congress Cataloging in Publication Data

Duffy, J   C
  Moot points.

  1. American wit and humor, Pictorial.   I.   Title.
NC1429.D748A4   1981   741.5'973   80-27228
ISBN 0-201-03968-0

Desert Rat

distorted self-image

One horse town

High Papal Turnover

Playing the devil's avocado.

(A very cheerful drawing)

(HOLDING THE CAMERA)

A gathering of goats

Hate Mail

H. P. WOOF
VICHYSSOISE BLDG.
GUERNSEY-ON-THAMES, N.M.

FIRST COW ON THE MOON!
"....domestic animals can be imported and a native meat supply will exist."
-Isaac Asimov
Sweet Jesus, this is no simple trek to the north forty!

Testing one's pen for stress in the desert.

A young man works against man and nature to retain a pair of mules....

The Happy Guy

Having lost the knack
for having fun.....

Defying Levity

PESKY MOOSE

PESKY MOOSE TWICE

Pesky Moose Thrice

· BITING THE HAND THAT FEEDS YOU.

YOUNG CHESTER MISTAKES A LIGHTBULB FOR AN IDEA.

startled by life's raw impact.

It is an imprudent priest
who dons bermudas
while suffering from a suspicious case
of rugburn of the knee

A highly sensitive cabbie overreacts to a bad inning by his fave-rave team in the ballgame on the radio....

The "Cold" of Monsieur Peuffe

Checking it twice

yearbook
pose

MR. MOOSKI

It is quite o.k. to seek out the comfort of strangers after swallowing salt water.....

Seasoned Veteran
(.....in violation of the Geneva Condiments.)

Tourist trap

The Woman Who Laughed With Mules!

Demonstrating a moose.

Deep lawn concern

This was no dream, thought Günther, correctly....

The woman
over whom men
lost their heads....

JOGGING WITH JEEZ

Why Vaudeville died.
MR. SMITH AND FREDERICK, THE CULTURED PIG

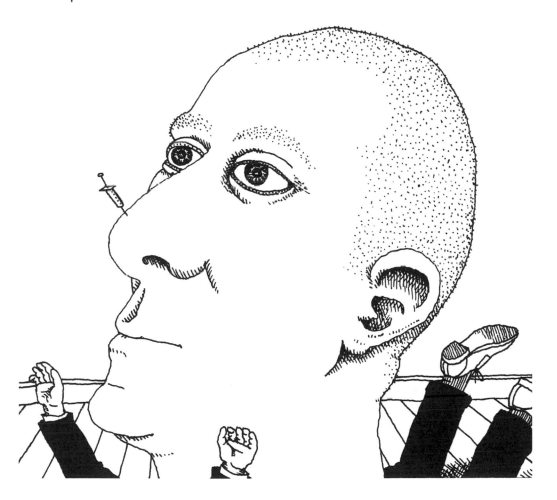

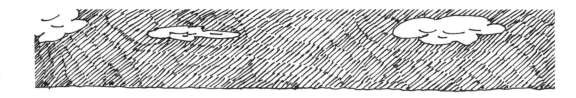

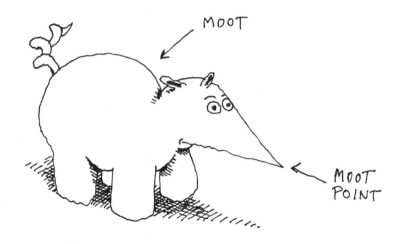

Farmer Bob and Ilsa, the literary cow....

BRAD DELIVERS HIS COPYRIGHTED "PAINFUL CHILDHOOD" MONOLOGUE, MOMENTS BEFORE IT IS PLACED IN PROPER PERSPECTIVE BY A FLOCK OF PREHISTORIC BOO-BOO BIRDS, INTENT ON NO GOOD.

(Traditionally, the best channel-swimmers are nude but standoffish.....)

Filing the preceding evening's nightmare (under "M" for mistake)

Alfred's civil question was met by Cybil's colorful "Shut up, Horse-lips" rejoinder once again.

This man is COMPLETELY BALD!!
This is his only way of making a living.
Will you help? Or will you simply turn the page?

YES! I WANT TO HELP!
HERE'S MY MONEY.

NAME _____
ADDRESS _____
CITY_____ STATE _____

COMPLETELY BALD
BOX 1500
DRAGON'S RUMP, N.J.

stray Guernsey in banana downpour, featuring God in his infinite Wizbang.

ILLEGAL ALIEN

The Calm Before The Strum

formerly "budding young French novelist" Hugo De Nez sets to work on what he hopes will be his greatest work, a letter to his landlord begging mercy.

Spain's legendary oppression-fighting heifer

The Miracle Of Conception

Through the looking-glass, stupidly

Word
Balloon
Salesman

Hörst Björst,
freelance Viking

When Irwin fell down, he grazed his niece.

The jaded priest and his happy dogs

Portrait of the artist as a young goose with shades.

A Firm Gripe On Reality

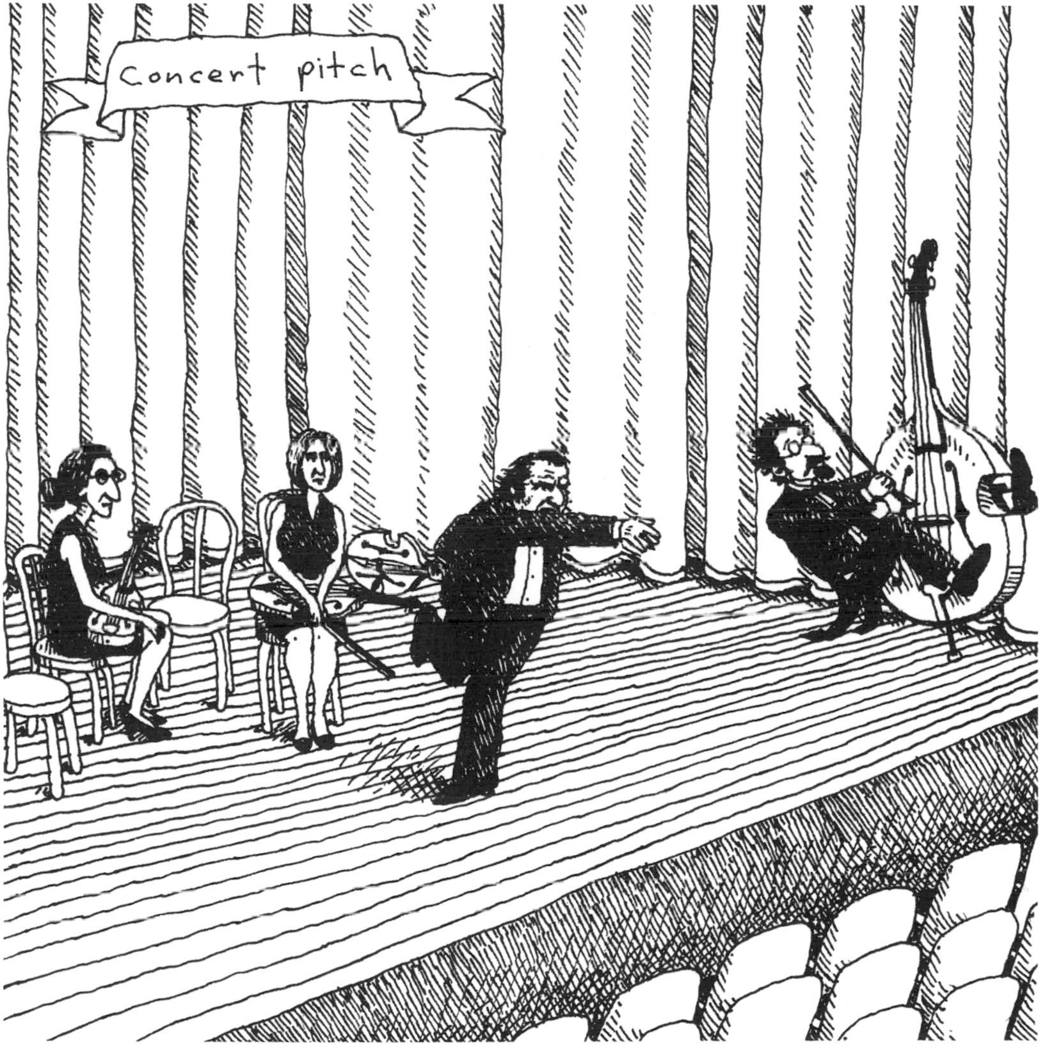
Concert pitch

Independently filthy

If you can draw

"Peppy, The Mysterious Animal"

YOU MAY HAVE
DEEPLY HIDDEN ART TALENT!

....send for free booklet!

"ART BE-CALMED MY LIFE. NOW I RAKE IN BUCKS INSTEAD OF THE STUPID LAWN."
-ALAN K.

"ONCE I COULD NOT DRAW A SIMPLE COW.... NOW I OWN THE HERD."
-JOAN R.

"ART KNOWLEDGE HAS BEEN A BOON. THE SENSITIVE LINGO DRAWS THE CHICKS LIKE A MAGNET."
-BOB W.

YET
ANOTHER
EXPERIMENT
VOLUNTEER
(AFTER)

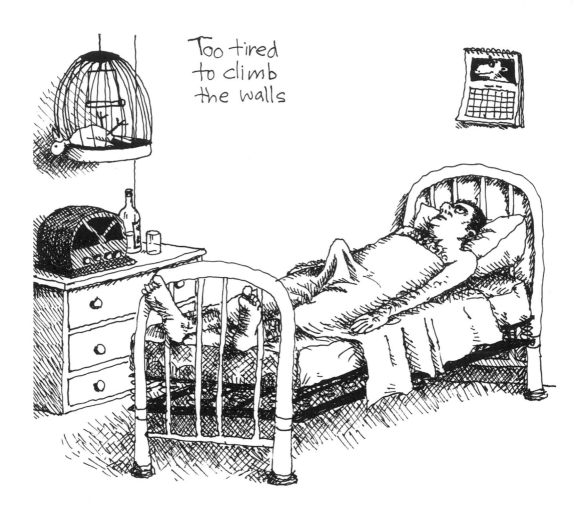

Too tired
to climb
the walls

Gentlemen Prefer
Blinds

The French have a word for it

Ronald the unstable stable-boy
watches his lunch slide under the door once again.

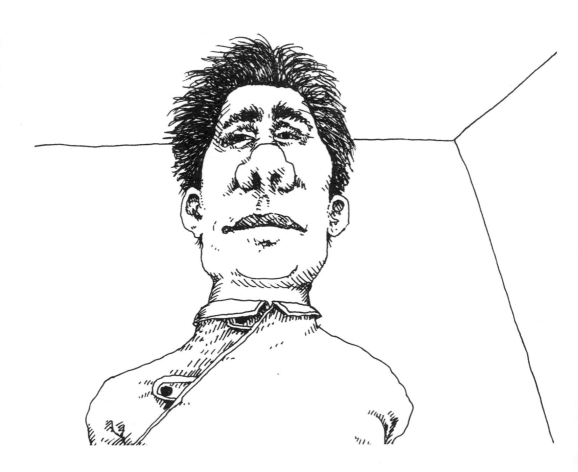

Too Hat to Hondle

humbled, and then some.

Every year when Ben's favorite season arrived, he would point it out to Hedwig.

Legendary Irish poet H.B. Eggs, suffering from writer's block, orders 19 consecutive glasses of prune nectar....

Coping with severe humor....

Walterweight

Dead men sell no shoes!

holding an all-night Virgil

The unparalleled camaraderie of desert yoga....

Tragedie Gymnastique

un

deux

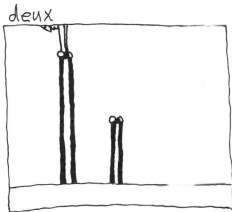

trois

quatre

They died with their bibs on.

Send your frustration
on vacation with new
CANNONBALL-
THRU-THE-WALL©

Steady as a rock,
and twice as smart

All About Art

J. C. Duffy was born sometime in the past, where he still spends much of his time.

Mr. Duffy, as he is known to his friend, is a former has-been and knows how to operate a jukebox. "I've been thrown out of better places than this!" he is fond of saying to no one in particular. He denies having political ambitions.

Mr. Duffy currently resides.